The ROGUE
River Guide

Kevin K. Tice

MOUNTAIN N'AIR BOOKS

Published by
Mountain N'Air Books
La Crescenta, CA 91224

Title: The Rogue River Guide
Copyright© in 1995 by Kevin Keith Tice

Published in the United States of America by
Mountain N'Air Books - P.O. Box 12540 - La Crescenta, CA 91224
Phone: (818) 951-4150, fax: (818) 951-4153

Cover design and book layout by Gilberto d'Urso
All photographs were taken by the author,unless otherwise credited.

ISBN: 1-879415-12-7

Table of Contents

A River Story

When I first started kayaking, I thought to run the Rogue River would be the apex of my paddling career. I had read descriptions of the river that left me with the impression that it required years of experience and considerable skill to successfully kayak the Rogue. I figured that a Rogue trip was several paddling seasons in the future. During my first season of paddling, I got the opportunity to participate in a trip on the Wild and Scenic Rogue. The trip was planned for late September, after the restricted permit season.

During that summer, we paddled as much as possible. Two, three, and sometimes four times a week we went to the local practice run to practice our ferries, eddy turns and all the other skills we had learned earlier that year. By the end of the summer, we were feeling pretty good, and eagerly anticipated our first multi-day river trip.

Finally the time for our trip arrived. We met our group at the Almeda Bar campground, and began loading the rafts and preparing our gear. Some of us went to shuttle the cars to the take out. Someone in our party said "follow me, I know the way," and off we went.

We wandered around on logging roads, and only after talking with a logger, were we able to determine where we were and how to get back to the river. Four hours later, we returned to Almeda Bar. After this less than successful shuttle attempt, we learned our lesson and had our cars shuttled for us.

With this auspicious beginning, I wondered about the paddling to come. First time jitters seemed amplified as I doubted our "leaders."

Once on the river, I realized that the paddling was going to be much easier than the logistics of the trip.

We had planned for a put-in time of about 12:00 o'clock. Because of our wonderful shuttle efforts, there were eight cars. It took some time to coordinate the trip back to the Galice store and arrange to have them shuttled. After all was done, we finally were ready to get into our boats and on the river. It was 2:30 or 3:00 when we actually got in the water.

The four miles of Class 2 water went easy. Some fun play spots along the way allowed us to warm up, get into the groove and in tune with the river. The butterflies, which had built up over the months of anticipation began to fade away, too. The easy rapids also allowed us to get acquainted with our new paddling partners, most of which we had never paddled with before.

Before too long, we passed under the bridge at Grave Creek. This signaled the approach of Grave Creek Rapid, and Grave Creek Falls.

Grave Creek went without incident, and Grave Creek Falls, which at some flows, (like the flow we were on) is a fairly good drop, proved interesting. This rapid was a ledge drop of about four feet, with a strange converging Vee-fold-hole-thing characteristic to it. I lined up right in the middle of the drop and took the plunge. Right at the moment that I did this, William Nealy's words and pictures from *Kayak* flashed in front of my eyes. In Nealy's words, this "confused mass of seething aeration" was gonna flip me faster than a New York minute. I thought to myself, "This really does look like a giant toilet flushing," and marveled at how the angle of the opposing flows exactly matched the angle of the bow of my boat. I was ready to get my ass kicked.

I completely submerged in the hole, and meanwhile threw out the best brace I knew. At the time, my bracing skills were way better than my confidence in my roll. I hung on tight, and blasted towards the surface like a breaching humpback whale. The 77 gallons of Infinity displacement rocketed me upwards. Blue sky and air told me that I was clear of Grave Creek Falls.

Soon we were upon Rainie Falls. The rafts promptly lined the Fish Ladder, and all the kayakers in the group either portaged, ran the Fish Ladder, or took the opportunity to scout the main falls. Of the thirteen kayakers in the group, four or five decided to go for it and run the main drop at Rainie. Tom, a tall, lanky guy, took his Lazer over the falls in exquisite style, and didn't even get his face wet. Corky, a big burly dude with a Corsica got trashed. He took the big drop, totally disappeared for what seemed an eternity, surfaced upside down, and rolled up with a look on his face that ran between confusion and terror. He paddled over to the group on shore with the simple comment of "I shouldn't have done that."

A couple of women in our group also ran the falls, and thought it was so much fun that they carried their boats back up again for another run of the falls. They too, had clean runs.

By this time it was getting late, and thought of finding a campsite came to front of the collective minds of the group. Most sites that we came to were already occupied, with most parties already preparing dinner. Because of our late star, we were looking at the possibility of finding only a marginal campsite.

We made camp in the dark, just above Tyee and Wildcat rapids. Spaghetti was to be the evening's dinner; what we got instead was pasta logs. The waterproof container wasn't. The spaghetti was one big ugly blob. Dinner was definitely not an Epicurean delight, and someone suggested that the fish in the river may appreciate it more than we would. Since we were tired and hungry, we carbo-loaded on spaghetti that more resembled string cheese than angel hair pasta, cleaned up, and went to bed.

The next morning, we learned an important lesson in minimum impact camping. More specifically, we learned what not to do. Apparently, someone decided that clean-up of the pasta logs was going to be difficult, and it would be easier if the lump of pasta in the pot soaked in the river over night. Upon inspection the next morning, we saw the widest variety of various river creatures—crawfish, small fish, snails, etc.—feasting upon the pasta. The left over spaghetti was dumped in the river as trout food. I am sure that other river travelers were not overly thrilled with the sight of pasta blobs floating down the river.

The next day was a long one, covering 16 miles. That morning, we put-in and immediately ran Wildcat and Tyee. The Howard Creek Chutes and Slim Pickens came next, and were easily negotiated. Upper Black Bar was next, and a quick scout showed the way. We stopped for lunch below Black Bar, and spent the next hour and a half working the endo spot. This playspot is probably the Rogue's most famous, and it lived up to its reputation of providing lots of air-time.

Somewhere along in Kelsey Canyon, the rafts and the kayaks got separated. We were delayed because one kayaker in the group, a woman with the same name as the drummer in the first rock power-trio super group of the sixties, took what seemed to be at least a hundred swims. Every drop meant a rescue of a swimmer and collection of gear.

Competition for camps is most intense at Mule Creek, since it is the last available campsite before Mule Creek Canyon and Blossom Bar, the two most difficult rapids that *must* be run. Again it was late in the day, and all sites were occupied at Mule Creek. We asked permission and set up our tents on the lawn at the Mule Creek Ranch. Dinner that night was some kind of Mexican stew-casserole creation. While tasty, it is probably best not to experiment too much with the menu on a river trip, lest there be some unintended pyrotechnic results, so to speak.

During the night we heard and saw many deer on the grass outside our tent. We quickly figured that the sounds from outside the tent were the deer grazing on the grass. It took a little longer to figure out that the really loud munching sounds were gophers under our tent. For several hours we smashed the mounds of dirt down as fast as they could push them up.

Tales of Mule Creek Canyon filled the conversation at breakfast. It was described as a wild place, full of big, unpredictable swirlys, boils, and strange currents. Blossom Bar was talked up as a class IV rapid that needed careful scouting, precise maneuvering, and clear focus.

We peeled out and headed for whatever challenge was ahead. Paddling stiffly at first, The Jaws indicated that Mule Creek Canyon was at hand. Remembering the words of our instructor, we kept a paddle blade in the water, hoping that our furious paddling would act as a brace and keep us upright. Mule Creek is a tight narrow, and full of unpredictable currents. I passed by my partner who was involuntarily surfing a big swirly. I think it is more appropriate to say (although she probably disagrees), that it was surfing her. A went by witnessing a flurry of low-braces, high-braces, and frenetic paddling. All those strokes worked, and soon we all regrouped at Stair Creek Falls. We also learned a good joke to pull on newcomers to the Rogue. After passing through Mule Creek Canyon, right when you hear the sound of Star Creek Falls, say something like "Now we get to go through the Coffee Pot!" Works every time.

Flatwater led to Blossom Bar. We pulled out on river right to scout and watch some other boats negotiate the rapid. Some in our group wanted to eat lunch first, but most of us said later, so we wouldn't have to stare in the face of our first class IV rapid for an hour before running it.

We scouted our line carefully, and decided to go for it. Four of us climbed into our boats looking for a successful run of Blossom Bar. We made the critical eddy by the big boulder, zipped down the big, glassy tongue, and then eddy-hopped the rest of the way through the rapid. After running this, we figured we were home free. Devil's Stairs was next, and after surfing a few waves, we pressed on to make camp for the night.

We found a camp somewhere along in the Brushy Bar-Solitude Bar area. Whatever was for dinner was not too memorable, as I cannot even remember what it was. This was the first night on the trip that we made camp in time to enjoy the evening. Some die-hards enjoyed a play wave right in front of our campsite well into the dark. And, contrary to all the dire warnings we had heard, Mr. Bear never came to visit us during the night.

The next day was a short one, with Clay Hill the only rapid of any significance. In the flatwater sections, we raised the sport of kayak jousting to new levels. For those unaware of kayak jousting, it is where you straddle your boat like a horse, just behind the cockpit. Then you try to knock over others riding their boats the same way. It's great fun.

Soon, we arrived at Foster Bar. Our cars were there, as the professional shuttlers were much better at it than we were, and we ended our trip with anticipation of our next Rogue trip. We broke down the rafts, loaded our cars, and headed home.

During our trip I learned of the outstanding beauty of the Rogue Canyon and its fun, exciting whitewater. I also realized that the Rogue was a special place for all that paddled its deep canyon. Since then the Rogue has become an annual trip.

The Rogue is an ideal river for a first multi-day river trip, whether it is raft supported, self-supported, or with an outfitter. Beginners make the trip in inflatable kayaks, and some kayak schools culminate their week long classes with a trip down the Rogue. The rapids are generally straight forward, and end in a pool for easy recovery. "User Friendly" is an apt description of the Rogue.

There are rivers that are more difficult technically, or may possess more beauty; what ever that may be, but few possess the combination of accessibility, fun rapids, and historical interest. These values are what make people come back to the Rogue year after year.

Are we having fun, yet!?

Be Careful

River sports can be dangerous. Accidents sometimes occur, resulting in monetary loss, injury, or even loss of life. This guidebook is only a description of features on the river—a detailed map. It cannot replace judgment, experience or skill.

Rivers and rapids change, and hazards may appear where none were before. Information contained in this book is believed to be accurate at the time that it was written, however changes in access, property ownership as well as the river itself may occur at any time. If in doubt, inquire locally, or of the managing agencies.

The author and the publishers of this guide do not assume any liability or responsibility of any sort for any loss. The final responsibility for a safe trip is always that of the individual.

How to Use this Guide

The guide focuses on the 34 mile Wild and Scenic Section of the Rogue, between the Grave Creek put-in and the Foster Bar take-out. Descriptions of rapids are intended to give an idea of what to expect, without being so detailed as to take away the adventure of discovery. As on any river, scout any rapid that you feel should be scouted. Almost everyone scouts Blossom Bar, and many scout Upper Black Bar the first time through.

Many parties put in at the Almeda Bar boat ramp, which often is less crowded than the Grave Creek put-in, and gives four miles of warm up before the standard put in at Grave Creek for the Wild and Scenic section of the Rogue. This section contains no rapids harder than class II. Other runs on the Rogue are described in the *Soggy Sneakers Guide,* and the *Rogue River Float Guide.*

River Difficulty

The majority of the Rogue's rapids are class II or Class III. The exceptions to this are Rainy Falls (V), and Blossom Bar (IV). There are easy alternatives to running Rainy Falls.

International Whitewater Rating Scale

Class I   Moving water, with a few riffles and small waves. Few or no obstructions. Easy.

Class II   Easy rapids with waves up to three feet, and wide, clear channels that are obvious without scouting. Some maneuvering is required.

Class III   Rapids with high, irregular waves. Rocks, waves, holes, and obstacles are more frequent and larger. Narrow passages often require complex maneuvering. Scouting may be required first time through. For closed boaters a reliable roll is highly recommended.

Class IV   Long, difficult rapids with constricted passages that may require precise maneuvering in very turbulent waters. For most boaters, scouting is a must. A reliable roll is essential, as rescues may be difficult.

Class V   Extremely difficult, long and very violent rapids with highly congested routes which nearly always must be scouted from shore. Rescue conditions are difficult and there is significant hazard to life in the event of a mishap. Ability to roll should be bomb proof.

Class VI   Difficulties of Class V carried to the extreme.

Class I "rapids" are not mentioned in this book, unless they are useful for location on the river or some other informative use.

Wild & Scenic River

The Rogue River was among the first group of rivers to be designated Wild and Scenic by Congress in the original Wild and Scenic Act of 1968. As a charter member, the Rogue is in an elite class of rivers, such as the Middle Fork Salmon, Lochsa, and Selway in Idaho, the Rio Grande in New Mexico, and Middle Fork Feather in California. Eighty four miles of the Rogue River was given protected status by its Wild & Scenic designation.

The Wild And Scenic Rivers Act prohibits dams or other projects sponsored by the federal government that would damage the river or local environs. Other protection is encouraged by zoning, public acquisition, and other means. The goal of Wild and Scenic designation is partially described in the Act itself;

"It is hereby declared to be the Policy of the United States that certain selected rivers of the Nation which, with their immediate environments, possess outstandingly remarkable scenic, recreational, geologic, fish and wildlife, historic, cultural values, shall be preserved in free-flowing condition, and that they and their immediate environments shall be protected for the benefit and enjoyment of present and future generations."

Wild and Scenic protection provides that the river corridor will not see future development. It cannot protect the river from many outside pressures, such as logging, road building or upstream development. America's rivers, including those already named in the Wild and Scenic protection, need continued care and stewardship from all of us who care about them.

Statistics

Put-in: Grave Creek: . . . . *625'*

Take out: Foster Bar: . . . . *150'*

Trip Length: . . . . *34 miles*

Average Gradient: . . . . *14 ft./mi.*

Trip Length: . . . . *2 to 5 days*

Maps:

U.S. Geological Survey 7.5" topographic maps: *Mt. Rueben, Bunker Creek, Kelsey Peak, Marial, Illahe.*

U.S. Forest Service: **Siskiyou National Forest, Kalmiopis Wilderness/Wild Rogue Wilderness**

Other maps: *Oregon Atlas & Gazetteer,* (DeLorme Mapping Company) are also available. This collection of topographic maps cover the entire state, and is a good source of information for points of interest and other features.

Flow Information

Recommended Flow:

1,000 to 6,000 cfs—Rogue River near Agness. Average summer time flows range from around 2,000 to 4,000 cfs.

Peak Recorded Flow: 290,000 cfs on December 23, 1964

The National Weather Service in Portland maintains a recording of river flows in Oregon. Call (503) 261-9246.

Since 1977 the flow on this section has been regulated by the Lost Creek dam, upstream of Grants Pass, Oregon.

Hydrograph

Monthly Mean. 1977 - 1993

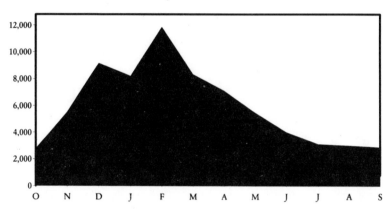

Mean Monthly Flow, Near the Agness , from 1977 to 1993											
	Oct.	Nov.	Dec.	Jan.	Feb.	Mar.	Apr.	May	June	July	Aug.	Sept.
1977	1598	**1659**	1555	1623	1550	2767	1479	2156	1293	934.6	896.9	1472
1978	1670	6517	**13720**	12210	13050	5215	5478	3660	2584	2492	1939	2128
1979	1482	1679	2671	4291	**7091**	5878	6346	7513	2297	2394	1866	1456
1980	2180	5041	8186	**16570**	6616	8180	7131	3985	2779	2223	1916	1346
1981	1486	2553	**8266**	3105	4953	3495	3294	2577	2140	2005	1936	1908
1982	2165	9253	**29250**	13340	16930	10500	15090	6174	4098	2779	2464	2352
1983	3497	4815	17010	11960	**30280**	17750	11820	8158	5021	3021	2910	3187
1984	2863	10070	**21940**	8069	12140	12100	9248	7365	5364	3446	3370	2816
1985	2512	**16650**	8780	3948	6334	4316	7656	3828	3147	2397	2412	2374
1986	2134	2632	4268	6672	**21820**	10380	3608	4493	2691	2439	2217	2521
1987	2137	4575	3560	**7360**	9611	7100	3316	2763	2180	2320	2245	1974
1988	1503	1386	5704	**7702**	3071	2207	2455	3230	3299	1829	1858	1630
1989	1421	5400	3629	7316	4546	**13510**	8651	5539	3241	2414	2515	2323
1990	2050	1977	2124	4676	**5616**	4729	3213	3182	3123	1879	2087	1900
1991	1672	1858	2432	3705	3591	**7108**	4541	5086	2873	2261	2071	1792
1992	1505	2089	3502	2839	**33872**	2048	2972	2124	1821	1339	1729	1676
1993	1481	2027	5264	9934	6771	10340	**10830**	7455	6292	3079	2710	2168
1994	Oct.	Nov.	Dec.	Jan.	Feb.	Mar.	Apr.	May	June	July	Aug.	Sept.
Mean	1,962	4,717	8,345	7,372	**11,050**	7,507	6,302	4,664	3,191	2,309	2,185	2,060
Max	3,497	16,650	29,250	16,570	33,872	17,750	15,090	8,158	6,292	3,446	3,370	3,187
Min	1,421	1,386	1,555	1,623	1,550	2,048	1,479	2,124	1,293	935	897	1,346

Weather and Climate

Prime season for a Rogue trip corresponds with the permit season from May through October. The weather during this time generally is quite comfortable. Daytime temperatures are commonly in the 70's and 80's, occasionally reaching 100°, while the nights are cool and damp, with the thermometer dropping to the 40's or 50's. Mornings can be foggy, even during the summer, but it usually burns off early, making way to sunny skies.

Coastal Oregon weather being what it is, rain is a possibility at anytime, but typically less than 10% of the annual precipitation falls during the summer months of June, July, and August. If you are planning a September or early October trip, watch the weather reports and forecasts carefully; you can minimize the risk of unexpectedly getting rained upon. The weather in Medford and Grants Pass gives a pretty good idea of what conditions to expect on the Wild and Scenic Rogue River. The National Weather Service maintains an office in Medford, which may be a useful reference.

Outside of the permit season, river use falls dramatically — the rain is almost assured to fall throughout the winter months, and snow is always a possibility. In exchange for the dreary weather, the off-season brings solitude and seclusion. During these times the only other river travelers likely to be encountered are fishermen.

Getting There

The Wild and Scenic Rogue River begins approximately 25 miles northwest of Grants Pass, in Southern Oregon. Commercial air service is available in Medford, about 30 miles east of Grants Pass. To reach the River, from Interstate 5, exit at Merlin (exit 61). Travel through Merlin to Galice, about 16 miles. If you're driving at night, watch for deer in the roadway.

One night on one of our trips–after watching our friend nearly plow over Bambi–I wrongly assumed that all deer had scattered from the roadway. I sped up, and nearly mowed down Bambi, also! Be careful out there!

Shuttle

The most direct shuttle route from Grave Creek to Foster Bar is as follows: Return to Galice, take Forest Service Road 34-8-36. This turns into Forest Service Road 23. Head towards Agness, through the tiny village of Illahe, and continue to Foster Bar. This route goes over a 5000 foot pass, and it is nearly 50 miles one way. Time of travel is about two hours. This route is often closed during the winter and early spring due to snow or poor weather conditions. This is the most popular route.

The winter route involves taking US-199 from Grants Pass to US-101, north to Gold Beach and then to Agness. One way distance is about 200 miles.

A third route exists as well. This route goes from exit 80 off I-5, over a number of Forest Service roads to Illahe and then to Foster Bar. This is a slow, narrow, winding paved gravel road. One way distance is about 82 miles between Galice and Foster Bar. The driving time is about four hours. See shuttle maps for more details. Check with the Forest Service, about accessibility and road conditions, before taking this route.

Shuttle Service

Galice Resort
11744 Galice Road
Galice, OR. 97532 (503) 476-3818

There are other shuttle services available, but I have personally used the Galice Resort shuttle service several times and found them very reliable. Certainly, the Galice Resort is the most convenient. In 1994 the cost to shuttle a car to Foster Bar was $50. Since the shuttle takes nearly four hours round trip and the road is tight, twisty and narrow, I'll always opt for the shuttle service.

Portage at Rainie Falls.

Shuttle Map
Galice to Foster Bar

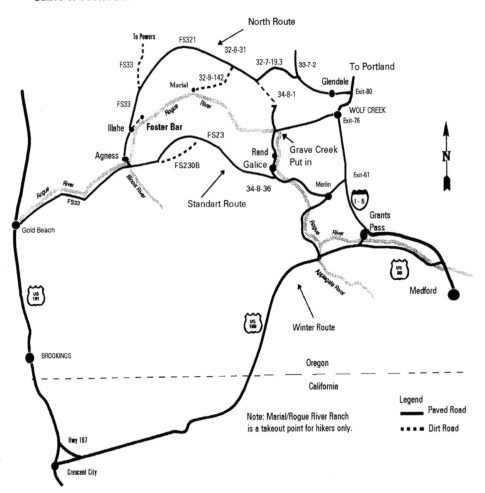

North Route

To Powers

FS321

32-8-31

FS33

32-7-19.3

33-7-2

To Portland

32-9-142

Glendale

Marial

34-8-1

Exit-80

FS33

WOLF CREEK

Rogue River

Exit-76

Illahe   Foster Bar

FS23

Rand

Grave Creek
Put in

Agness

FS230B

Galice

Exit-61

Illinois River

34-8-36

Merlin

I-5

Rogue River

Rogue River

FS33

Standart Route

Grants
Pass

Gold Beach

Rogue River

US 99

US 101

Applegate River

Medford

US 199

Winter Route

BROOKINGS

Oregon

California

Legend

Hwy 197

Note: Marial/Rogue River Ranch
is a takeout point for hikers only.

Paved Road

Crescent City

Dirt Road

River Courtesy

The Rogue provides a getaway for many users and types of craft. We all have a responsibility to get along and be courteous to each other. Rafters, kayakers, fishermen and jet boats all use the river and present challenges for all to be considerate of each other.

Most obviously, avoid getting too close to fishermen's lines. Most guides use the McKenzie style drift boats, which means that people are fishing while drifting. Less obvious, is that in some rapids or riffles, the guide will ferry or pull against the current to maximize drift time in the particular riffle. One time, I was following a McKenzie too close, flipped, and nearly got hooked and tangled with the fisherman's line. Be sure to allow plenty of space to allow for the slower moving drift boats.

Unlike some Western rivers, such as the Middle Fork Salmon in Idaho, campsites on the Rogue are not assigned. It is strictly first-come, first-served. Because of this, competition for campsites can get intense, especially late in the day or at places like Mule Creek.

Sometimes campsites have to be shared; make the best of it. For self-support kayakers, sharing a site can mean the difference between ramen noodles or a grilled steak dinner. Certainly, sharing a site with a rafting party should at least score a cold beer or two. Be friendly and helpful on the river to each other; it almost always comes back to you.

On a recent trip we shared our perfect gravel beach with a party from the Portland area. Earlier that day, we had run into them when they needed a screwdriver to fix an oarlock. I offered my Swiss Army knife and in exchange they gave us a couple of cold beers. Late in the afternoon we again saw them when they asked if we would share our beach. We said sure.

Apparently, they felt sorry for us and offered all kinds of food that night. We were quite satisfied with our meal cooked on the MSR stove, but appreciated the offer. The next morning, however, we did take them up on their offer of bacon, eggs, and hot coffee. Contrast this story with the following story on another trip.

Early one morning I was up before the rest of my group, enjoying the view of the fog and mist swirling off the still water and around the low rock cliffs near Jenny Creek. I saw a raft drift around the corner, and thought to myself "Gee, those guys are ambitious, getting such an early start! ," as it was not even 7:00 a.m. yet. Then I realized that *nobody* was getting an early start as the raft was drifting without the benefit of an oarsman.

I quickly jumped in my kayak, and towed the errant raft back to shore. When I got to shore, the others in my group had waken, and we all had a good laugh about my newly found boat.

We were quite considerate; we drank only a couple of the beers that we found in the cooler (it was still early) and took turns rowing back and forth across the river. We laughed some more about the poor, hapless fool that didn't tie his boat up too well, and how the people in his group must be completely *thrilled* with their boat being gone. By this time they probably were all thinking about the long hike out to the cars. With some duct tape we modified the manufacturer's name plate on the raft—we carefully blocked out the letter "C" in the name *Incept.*

After 30 minutes or so, around the corner came a guy paddling like a bat out of hell, on a sit-on-top kayak. We laughed some more when we realized it was a *Yahoo* kayak he was paddling. Somehow, it seemed quite appropriate.

Anyway, the guy thanked us profusely, and promised to give us all the beer we wanted throughout the day. We gave him back his boat, and off he went. We never saw his group at all that day, until very late near Half Moon Bar.

It was near 5:00 p.m. and we still had not found our campsite for the night. To save time, we had run Blossom Bar without scouting, as we figured that we could save nearly an hour that way. Finally, we found a place that looked promising, and got the group moving towards what we thought would be our spot for the night.

As we made our way towards the shore, one of the kayakers from the ghost-raft group came charging up to the beach, jumped out of his boat, and very loudly proclaimed the spot to be his.

We had a group conference, and decided it wasn't worth a confrontation. While we grumbled to ourselves about saving their boat and what ingrates they were, we shrugged our shoulders, got back in our boats and found a campsite just downstream in Huggins Canyon, and all was well.

Kayakers and canoers should be conscious about playing in spots hidden from upstream traffic, and stopping to catch surf waves with traffic behind. Use common sense.

Jet Boats will be encountered from about Devil's Stairs Rapid to the take out. These boats deserve special attention for a couple of reasons; they're real big, and real fast. Some of these boats are 40 passenger beasts, and travel upstream at 30 miles per hour.

Ordinarily, downstream traffic has the right of way over traffic moving upstream. An important exception to this is jet boats under power, climbing up a rapid. Once a jet boat starts up a rapid, it can't stop. In this circumstance, wait until the jet boat is through the rapid, then proceed. While these boats draw just inches of water, they do require a clear channel to navigate. Give them plenty of room.

Jet Boats are part of the history of the Rogue, and in spite of the loud noise, they can be entertaining. The tourists on the boats coming up from the coast are generally friendly, and are thrilled to see kayakers. They will take snapshots and video tapes to show to the folks back home.

These boats can throw quite a wake and are fun to surf behind. Generally the pilots are quite cooperative if you show them your intention to surf the wake.

Permits

Use is regulated on the Rogue River; a permit is required. New regulations went into effect for the 1995 season, along with a new application process. The Forest Service has contracted with Tioga Resources, Inc., of Roseburg, Oregon to conduct the permit lottery application process. Since 1995 is the first year under this system, contact the river information office for any new rules or regulations.

The use of the river is restricted from May 15 through October 15. This is an extension of the regulated, limited use period of the past, and was made in response to the large number of people using the river before and just after the permit season. In the past, on the weekends following the end of the permit season, use of the river was as high as three hundred people per launch day. Use through out the permit season is limited to one hundred and twenty people per launch day, including commercial users.

The permit application process is chock-full of specifics, and full of opportunities for disqualification. Be sure to follow the rules. Particularly important is that *your name can appear in the lottery only once.* You cannot apply for more than one launch date in the lottery, and if you are applying as a trip leader, you cannot be listed as an alternate trip leader on any other application. Apparently this restriction does not prohibit you from requesting another permit in the "Open Pool" period for permit dates either canceled or not filled during the lottery.

One last word regarding *"no-shows."* The managing authorities take a dim view if you fail to pick up your permit after it has been confirmed. Certain penalties have been put into place to encourage compliance with the rules. First, the $10 per person processing fee paid upon confirmation is forfeited, and second, you are prohibited from being a trip leader (or an alternate) for the remainder of the current permit season, or the entire next permit's season period.

Application Period

Applications will be accepted between December 1 and January 31. While postmark date has no effect upon your chance of success, applications with postmarks before or after these dates will be rejected.

Where to Apply

Mail your application to TRI, P.O. Box 5149, Roseburg, Oregon 97470.

All applications must be mailed to this address. Don't send your application to the River Information Office or any other address.

You may also fax your application to:

TRI at (503) 672-4168.

Notification

Successful applicants will be notified by mail on March 1.

Age Requirement

Applicants must be at least 18 years old on or before the launch date.

Picture Identification

A picture ID is required to get your permit on launch day.

Open Pool

For launch dates still open after the lottery, or early cancellations, an "open pool" period exists. Permits are available on a first come, first served basis. Call the River Information Office, (503) 672-4168 starting April 1, for these permits.

Application Form

Applications for a permit must be made on a 3"x 5" index card. Submissions of any other size or not on card stock will be disqualified. Your application must contain the following information:

Party Size:

Indicate a specific party size for your application. The maximum party size allowed is 20. Try to be realistic estimating your party size; generally, smaller groups are more successfull in the lottery.

Launch Date:

This is the specific date you want for your put-in date. Note that there is no provision for an alternate launch date.

Party Leader:

Your name, address, and phone number.

Alternate Leader

An Alternate Leader may be named at the time your application is made. The Alternate Leader is the only person who can use the launch permit if the original Party Leader cannot use the permit. If the Party Leader is not able to make the river trip, and there is no alternative named, you cannot trade, sell, or give away your permit. The only alternative is to cancel the trip.

Signature

The Party Leader must sign the application.

Format Summary

3"x5" index card with the following information:

Top Left Corner-One specific Launch date.

Top Right Corner-Specific party size, no larger than 20.

Left Body-Party Leader name, address, and phone number.

Lower Left Body-Alternate Party leader, address, and telephone number. (This step is optional)

Bottom Left-Party Leader signature.

A completed example of a permit application is shown below.

Fees

You must include a non-refundable $3.75 application fee with your permit request. For successful applicants, a $10.00 per person fee must be paid for the "administration" of this public resource. This fee must be paid when confirming the permit with the Forest Service, and is non-refundable in the event of a *"no-show"* or cancellation. Do not miss the confirmatin date, as this too will lead to the loss of your permit. You **must confirm** your permit at least ten days before the permit date.

Sample of a permit request on a 3"x5" card.

mm/dd/yy   *8*

Swimmer, Bob
456 Coldwater Street
Drain, OR 97500

Alternate Leader's Name
2 Banana Rd.
Drain, OR 97500

Leader's Signature

Regulations

Compared to other Western Rivers, the regulations on the Rogue regarding fires, sanitation and the like are fairly simple. The summary of regulations here is current as of October 1994.

Fire pans are required at all times during the year, for any open fire within 400 feet of the river. The authorities do not specify any particular requirements for fire pans, as long as they fulfill the spirit and intent of the regulations: Keep the beaches clean and keep the rocks unscarred. Pack out all ashes.

If you have a fire, use only dead and down wood. Don't use snags or other standing, dead wood.

Check at the River Information Office for any special regulations or fire restrictions during times of high fire hazard.

Sanitation

Currently there are no regulations that require the carry-out of human waste. When technology and money permit the construction of sanitation facilities at the Forest Bar take-out, a carry out policy will take effect. The Rogue has the highest toilet-per-mile ratio of any of the rivers in the Western United States that require a use permit, so it is pretty easy to avoid most problems by using the facilities provided.

If you camp at a site where there is no toilet, use common sense, and an overriding concern about the next camp user when determining where to make your outdoor "depository." Current rules forbid the use of the sand or gravel beaches below the high-water mark to dispose of human waste, for either liquid or solid matter. You should dig a hole 6" to 8" deep, well above the high water line, and far from potential campsites. When you are done, fill in the hole, and CARRY OUT THE TOILET PAPER. Do not try to burn the paper, nor bury it, because sure as shit, some animal will dig it up and make a lovely "toilet paper garden." The same rules apply to liquid waste.

The sand and gravel beaches do not contain the needed bacteria for biodegradation, so anything left here will lend a "kitty-litter" aroma to the campsite. It seems to me that while it is not an official policy, it really could not hurt to pee directly into the river, like in the Grand Canyon. If you prefer a handy bush to the river, make sure it is far away from any potential campsite or sleeping area.

Hopefully, if we all voluntarily make a commitment to proper human waste management in the river corridor, more restrictive rules won't have to be enacted. Even in the absence of a carry-out policy, we should use our own carry-out standard, if at all possible. If we don't, eventually even self-support kayak groups will have to carry an "approved toilet," something that would be very awkward at best. It is possible a policy could be so restrictive as to effectively eliminate the possibility of self-support kayak trips.

Make the effort to inform others about this problem and to leave a clean river corridor. It can only help in the long run.

Guides and Outfitters

Oregon State Law requires that individuals accepting fees for guide or outfitting services be registered with the Oregon Marine Board, and carry proper insurance coverage.

Apparently, they take this very seriously, as the State's brochure on this topic says to report any illegal guiding activities to the State Police on their Hotline! See page 60 for list of approved river running outfitters.

Self support group organizing gear at the Alameda Bar put-in

Phil and Janet below Blossom Bar

A Mile by Mile Guide

These descriptions are for normal summer time flows.

RAPIDS	Miles from Grave Creek	Miles to Foster Bar
Grave Creek Boat Ramp	0.0	34.2
Grave Creek (III)	0.0	34.2
Grave Creek Falls (III)	0.3	33.9
Sanderson Island (II)		
Rainie Falls (V)	1.7	32.5

Grave Creek Boat Ramp
This is the most popular put-in, and it can be quite crowded at times. Several trash cans and pit toilets are provided, but there is no available drinking water at this location. Take advantage of the facilities. This is the last chance for dumping of any trash until Foster Bar.

Grave Creek (III)
Less than 100 yards from the put-in, the boater is in this straight forward rapid which is easily boat scouted. Near the bottom of this drop is a hidden midstream boulder. Pass to the left of it.

Grave Creek Falls (III)
This rapid is a sharp drop, followed by a good pool for recovery, collecting gear, etc. The best run is left of the rock in the middle of the river.

Sanderson Island (II)
The river splits around an island here. At the head of this island is a fun low water play spot.

Rainie Falls (V)
This is the biggest rapid on this section of the Rogue. It is hard to miss. The river canyon opens up slightly here, and during busy summer weekends there is lots

RAPIDS	Miles from Grave Creek	Miles to Foster Bar

of activity. There is a large eddy and a trail on river left for scouting or for the easiest view of the falls. The left side also offers a quick, short portage route for kayakers. Otherwise, pull out on river right to portage or line.

This rapid has alternatives to running the main falls, a 12 to 15 foot waterfall. On the far right, the Fish Ladder offers the most popular way around the falls. This class II chute is easy, and depending on the water level, can be a real bottom scraper. Most rafters line and or scrape their way down this, so it can be quicker for kayakers just to shoulder their boats and walk around, using the trail through the grass.

The middle route is a Class IV staircase drop. This drop involves an interesting entry, close to the main falls. At higher flows this is an option for those looking for more thrills. Scout this route carefully, (particularly the entrance) as it involves a move precariously close to the gnarliest portion of the main falls.

Rainie Falls proper is Class V. It is a big drop into a big reversal. I've seen this drop cleanly boofed, and I've seen people get munched, too. It was interesting to watch a Corsica disappear for what seemed to be a long time in the froth. It was described as a "radical washing machine under there!". For those inclined to run this drop, they don't need instructions on the how to. Be aware however that there are stories of metal debris in the base of these falls, making a low water run more dangerous.

China Gulch (II)   2.2   32.0

China Creek enters on the left. About a mile of flatwater follows this rapid.

Whiskey Creek enters on the right, Rum Creek enters on the left. Flatwater and some easy riffles continue for another mile or so.

An upstream view at Rainie Falls.

Playspot below Slim Pickens rapid.

RAPIDS	Miles from Grave Creek	Miles to Foster Bar
Tyee Rapids (III)	4.4	29.8
Wildcat (III)	4.8	29.4
Russian (II)	5.2	29.0
Upper Montgomery (II)	5.5	28.7
Lower Montgomery(II)		
Howard Creek Chutes(II)	6.1	28.1
Slim Pickens (III)	6.9	27.3
Washboard Rapids (II+)	7.2	27.0

Tyee Rapids (III)
Identify this rapid by the low rock outcroppings on river right, as well a large rock mid-channel. The right side is the preferred channel. At lower flows there's a big, but crashable hole in the middle of this rapid.

Wildcat (III)
The river splits around an island; the main channel is on the right. This rapid consists of straight forward waves and holes, then makes a sharp turn at the bottom

Russian (II)

Upper Montgomery (II)

Lower Montgomery(II)

Howard Creek Chutes(II)
A series of three drops and chutes. At the end of this series, Howard Creek enters on the left, a nice pool is just a short hike upstream.

Slim Pickens (III)
At all but the lowest levels, kayaks and canoes can pass either side of the big rock, but the right side is the more interesting and fun choice. For rafts and drift boats it is a tight squeeze, hence its name. Look for the old metal barge at the top of this rapid on river left. It was washed here in 1955. At low flows there is a good play spot at the bottom of this drop.

Washboard Rapids (II+)
Two sharp narrow chutes.

RAPIDS	Miles from Grave Creek	Miles to Foster Bar
Plowshare (II+)	7.7	26.5
Big Windy(II)	8.0	26.2
Windy Creek Chutes (II)	8.1	26.1

Windy Creek Chutes (II)
Bunker Creek enters on the right. Big Windy creek enters the Rogue about 50 yards downstream on the left.

Upper Black Bar (III)   8.5   25.7
The standard run is river right, close to the rock wall. The center and left side is full of rocks and holes. Through trial and error, it has been proven that it is possible to paddle and/or swim down the middle of this rapid (I can't think of any particular reason why you would want to). Towards the bottom of the rapid is probably the Rogue's most famous play spot. A pourover center right provides an excellent ender spot, with a good eddy. Scout on river right.

Lower Black Bar (II+)   8.6   25.6
A smooth, glassy tongue drops into standing waves.

Black Bar   8.8   25.4
Above here is Black Bar Lodge.

Little Windy (II)   9.3   24.9
Little Windy Creek enters river left.

Jenny Creek   10.1   24.1
Flows in on left, with good campsites both above and below the creek.

Horseshoe Bend (III)   10.4   23.8
The river makes a big right hand bend. Class II waves lead to a rock wall on the left, where bigger reaction waves bounce and bend off the rocks. At low water watch for an undercut wall. It is tempting to sneak this bend

RAPIDS	Miles from Grave Creek	Miles to Foster Bar

on the right in the eddy, but the eddy is full of funky upwelling water. Just past this, the river bends to the left.

Horseshoe Bend campground on the right	10.5	23.7
Meadow Creek and campground on river right	11.5	22.7
Dulog Creek	11.9	22.3

Enters on the left. A short hike up the creek leads to a sculpted rock pool.

Kelsey Canyon	12.2	22.0

For the next mile the canyon narrows, and several class II drops make for one of the best sections of the trip. The scenery here is excellent, as numerous class II drops proceed in quick succession in the narrow canyon.

Kelsey Falls (II+)	12.6	21.6
Kelsey Creek	13.0	21.2

Enters on the left.

Battle Bar	13.9	20.3

The site of a skirmish between the Rogue Indians and the Army. Above the river on the left, look for the old cabin. This cabin can provide adequate shelter during bad weather.

Winkle Bar	15.2	19.0

Hewitt Creek enters on the left. Across the river is Winkle Bar. A short hike leads to Zane Grey's cabin. Winkle Bar often works out as a good lunch stop, and the cabin is an interesting side trip. At the end of Winkle Bar, a mid-stream rock has a big pillow, and can make for a good spot for splats and other fun things.

RAPIDS	Miles from Grave Creek	Miles to Foster Bar
Missouri Creek Enters on the left.	16.0	18.2
Quail Creek Burn River left. This is the location of a fire in 1970. A portion of this burned again in 1994.	16.4	17.8
Long Gulch (II)	17.3	16.9
Big Boulder (II)	17.6	16.6
Island Rapids (II)	17.8	16.4
Johns (II)	18.0	16.2
Maggies (II)	18.4	15.8
China Bar Rapids (II) Flat water marks Rogue River Ranch, Mule Creek and the Mule Creek campgrounds.	19.1	15.1
Marial Lodge. High on river right.	19.7	14.5
Mule Creek Canyon (III)	19.8	14.4

Two large rocks (The Jaws) block the right side of the river and mark the entrance to Mule Creek Canyon. Pass these rocks on the left. The canyon narrows and the gradient picks up. A series of class III rapids swing first right, then left, then back to the right. Along the left side of the canyon wall are some rocks, which either make ugly pourovers at low water or holes at higher flows. Mule Creek Canyon is probably the most spectacular section of this part of the Rogue. This is a great class III section. At some flows there is some good surfing waves in the early sections of the canyon. These waves can also provide good endo launching points. You'll have to catch these play spots on the fly, as there is no easy place to eddy out in here.

RAPIDS	Miles from Grave Creek	Miles to Foster Bar

Coffee Pot (III)   19.8   14.4

The water settles down briefly, turns a corner and flows into Coffee Pot. The river squeezes down to only about 15 feet, (The Narrows) as it twists, swirls and boils. The secret here for the boater in doubt is to paddle like crazy! The hydraulics here are big, weird, swirly, and fun! Be sure to leave plenty of time for big boats (rafts and drift boats) to pass through here, because they can either pass right through, or spin around, stuck for awhile. There's really no way to see if they are through. If you get in here with a raft, you're probably gonna get munched. As one rafting friend said, "Control has nothing to do with getting through Mule Creek Canyon!" This section is one of the best on the entire river. Be sure to enjoy the scenery, whether in your boat or out of it.

Mule Creek Canyon and the Coffee Pot can be most intimidating part of the Rogue. To be sure, the hydraulics in here are pretty wild, but don't be put off by all the hype.

On one trip, it was only the sixth time on the river for one of our buddies, but because of his athletic ability and great attitude, we felt that with a little guidance, he could do just fine. I told him that Mule Creek may be some of the hardest paddling on the river, but even if he did swim, he should enjoy the view, and we would be close by for moral support until the end of the canyon, because there were no easy spots to get back into a boat.

In the first series of class III rapids, we had a swimmer. With boat in one hand and paddle in the other, there wasn't too much to do other than ride it out. I eddied out in one of the small niches in the rock wall, and looked upstream to see Phil with a goofy grin on his face, spinning round and round in a big swirly, saying "Yippee!! Whee!!"

At lower water levels there is a calm section just before the Coffee Pot. Here, Phil got back into his boat, and we waited for a raft that was coming through to pass. While we waited, I said that I thought we were through the big stuff, and the rest was easy. I was wrong. We hadn't yet gone through the Coffee Pot.

After what we thought was enough time for the raft to get through, we peeled out. Rounding the corner, we knew we were hosed. Ahead was the Coffee Pot, and the raft bouncing from wall to wall. We did what we could to slow down and make some space, but to no avail.Phil got munched by the raft and swam again. I squeezed by the raft with the narrowest of margins. At the big pool below Stair Creek Falls we regrouped and met the rafters we shared the canyon with. At this time we figured out why the raft was having such a hard time bouncing through the Coffee Pot. The floor of the raft was littered with empty 22 ounce cans of Foster's Lager.

RAPIDS	Miles from Grave Creek	Miles to Foster Bar
Stair Creek Falls	21.3	12.9

Enters on the left at the end of Mule Creek Canyon. This is a worthwhile stop. A hike upstream leads to a miniature Mule Creek Canyon After this, some flat water leads to Blossom Bar.

Blossom Bar (IV)	22.6	11.6

Blossom Bar is recognized by the scores of boulders which clog the river. Pull out and scout this rapid on river right. At typical summertime flows this rapid is well within reach for the class III paddler. This rapid can be portaged, but with some difficulty. If you decide to walk around this rapid, see if another boater in your group will walk back up

RAPIDS	Miles from Grave Creek	Miles to Foster Bar

and run your boat through, because carrying a boat around this is fairly strenuous.

The standard run through this rapid is as follows: Enter far left, and eddy out behind the large rocks in the center of the river. This will put you above and to the right of the Picket Fence. Work right and ride the tongue into the second half of the rapid. Eddy hop or work towards the left, passing the 'Volkswagen' rock on your right.

Devils Stairs (III) — 22.9 — 11.3

Around the corner from Blossom Bar, this rapid starts off as a slide into a wave train, and then slams into a rock wall protruding from the right bank. Good surf/play waves here. The eddy on the left has a fairly strong recirculating flow, with a weird cross-flow. We rescued an open canoer (name withheld to protect the guilty) here once. Without a tow system, it was a real Chinese fire drill with four kayakers trying to bulldoze a canoe and get a swimmer to shore. From this point downstream, watch for jet boats.

Gleason Bar — 23.1 — 11.1
Left Bank

Paradise Creek — 23.4 — 10.8
Enters on the right. Hike upstream to a pool near the trail.

Paradise Lodge — 23.7 — 10.5
Located high above the river on the right. In the flood of 1964, rising water reached all the way to the lodge.

Paradise Bar — 24.3 — 9.9
On the right. Several campsites here.

Half Moon Bar — 24.3 — 9.9
lodge on the left, above the river

RAPIDS	Miles from Grave Creek	Miles to Foster Bar
Rapid(II)	24.4	9.8
Huggins Canyon	25.0	9.2

This is a stretch of about a mile of flat water. Rock walls make for great scenery—look for California Fuchsia.

East Creek	26.1	8.1

Enters on river left. Steep rock steps lead to the site of an old cabin, long since gone. All that remains is a foundation and the chimney.

Brushy Bar	26.3	7.9
Brushy Bar Creek	26.3	7.9
Tichenor Riffle (II)	26.8	7.4

Many campsites on river right over the next third of a mile.

Solitude Riffle (II)	27.1	7.1

Decision Rock marks the end of this easy rapid.

Tate Creek	28.2	6.0

Enters on the right. A short hike up the creek leads to the famous Tate Creek Slide, a natural waterslide. Two campsites are available here, one on each side of the creek.

Tacoma Camp	28.3	5.9

Campsite on river right.

Tacoma Rapid (II)	28.7	5.5
Clay Hill Lodge	28.9	5.3

River Right. Look for the dinosaur tree.

Clay Hill (III)	29.1	5.1

This rapid starts with some class II water and then turns sharply left over a gravel bar slide (stay left here). At low water the far right side is a jumble of boulders.

RAPIDS	Miles from Grave Creek	Miles to Foster Bar

There are good play waves in this rapid; work them for all they're worth because this about the last play spot before the take out.

Clay Hill Stillwater	29.4	4.8

Flatwater for the next two miles. Often a breeze blows upstream in the afternoon, making this section somewhat of a drag. The scenery does make up for it however, as the geology makes a significant change. The rocks here are a dark conglomerate which have been eroded in places to form sculpted caves and potholes.

Fall Creek	30.2	4.0

Enters river left. A small waterfall is just upstream

Flora Dell Creek	30.5	3.7

On river right. Two rock pools are a short hike up this creek.

Payton Riffle (II)	31.1	3.1
Wild River Lodge	31.2	3.0

On the left bank

Burnt Rapids (II)	32.0	2.2
Watson Creek	32.4	1.8

Enters river left. This marks the end of the Wild & Scenic segment of the river. From here to the take out, the river is only "scenic."

Rapid (II)	32.6	1.6
Big Bend	32.7	1.5

The Rogue makes a big turn and heads due south at this point.

Brewery Hole (II)	33.4	1.0

Named for the beer like suds that sometimes accumulate here.

RAPIDS	Miles from Grave Creek	Miles to Foster Bar
Billings Creek and Illahe Lodge on river right.	33.7	0.5
Foster Creek enters river right.		
Foster Bar	34.2	0.00

Foster Bar

River Right. This is the take-out. Boat ramp, parking lot, trash and recycling facilities.

Dispose of your trash appropriately, making use of the recycling containers. Check the parking area, one more time before departing, for anything you may be leaving behind.

Clay Hill Rapids. The last good playspot before the take-out

RIVER MAP: Grave Creek to Meadow Creek

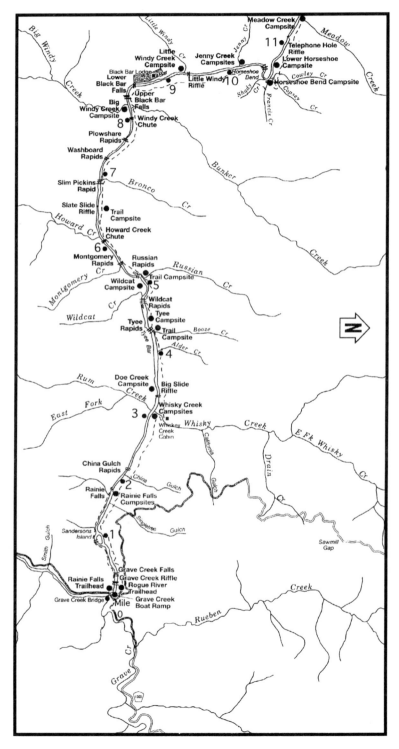

RIVER MAP: Black Bar to Mule Creek

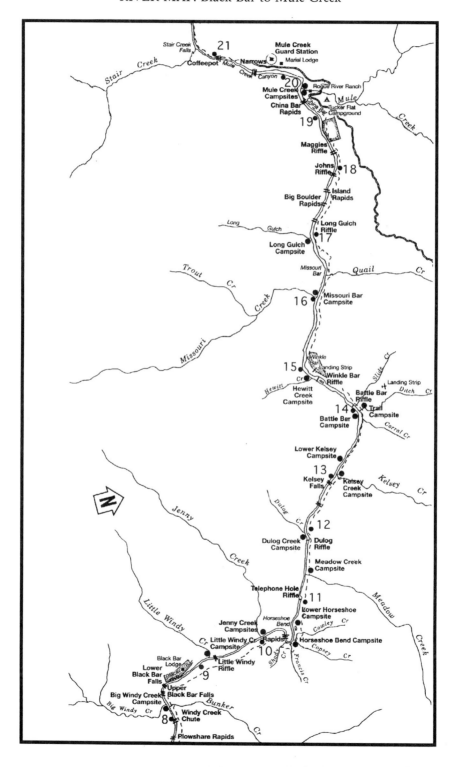

RIVER MAP: Mule Creek to Watson Creek

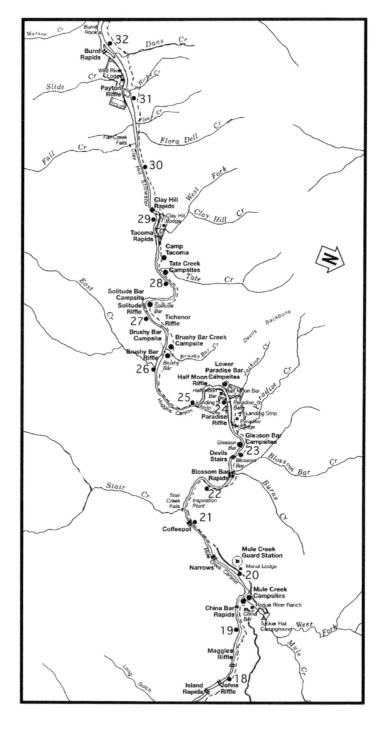

RIVER MAP: Clay Hill Stillwater to Foster Bar Take-out

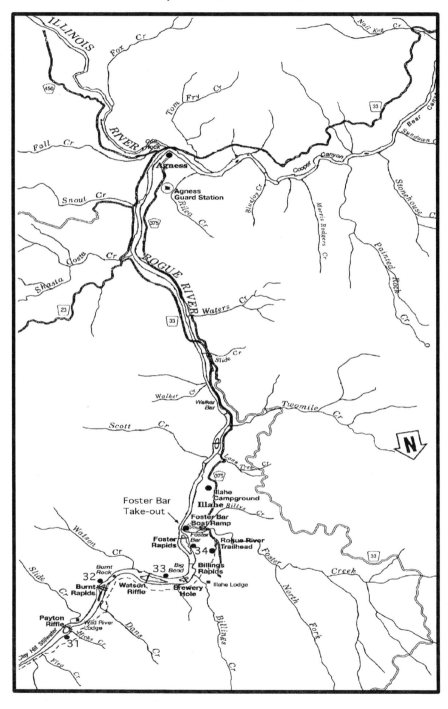

Points of Historical Interest

Whiskey Creek Cabin

This well preserved cabin, built by miners in the 1800's was called home by a variety of people over the years. The last known resident was a fellow named Si Whiteneck. Si lived in the cabin in 1915, when Glen Wooldrige made his first boat trip down the river. Apparently he was quite a chef, and cooked for CCC and Forest Service crews when they were in the area.

Whiskey Creek, and nearby Rum and Booze creeks were named by early gold miners that must have had other things on their minds, besides panning and digging for gold. Another interesting note is that Rainie Falls was known for a while as Whiskey Creek Falls. The name of the falls was changed later for Old Man Ramey, an early day curmudgeon who lived down at China Gulch, and gaffed salmon at the falls.

Zane Grey Cabin

The famous novelist Zane Grey was one of the most prominent visitors to the Rogue Canyon. Drawn to the Rogue by the great fishing in the 1919, in 1925 he began to make regular trips on the Rogue and came to enjoy the river so much as to build a log cabin at Winkle Bar for a second home.

Initially, Grey made the downriver trip without his wife, who stayed in a hotel in Grants Pass while he was fishing and writing. Later, when train service reached the West Fork, and a good pack trail was built from there to the Rouge river, she began to travel with him to Winkle Bar.

Two books, Tales of Freshwater Fishing, and Rogue River Feud, were written using the Rogue as a backdrop. The Rogue River Feud is the best known of the two novels, and is said to be based on a local conflict between the seine netters of the lower river, and the gillnetters of the upper river near Grants Pass.

The upstream gillnetters accused the seiners of taking all the fish downstream, and that fish belonged to them. Ultimately there was a scuffle between two men, one from each group. One of them brought charges of assault and battery against the other. The court order the offender to pay a fine and court costs totaling nine dollar to the injured party. And this is said to be the origin of the story told in the Rogue River Feud.

Visitors are welcome at the cabin at Winkle Bar. This is privite property and the current owners request visitors not to picnic on the grounds.

Beside the log cabin there is one of the boats used by Grey during his 1925 trips.

Zane Grey's Log Cabin

Battle Bar Cabin

There is not much left of this old cabin, the walls are gone, only the roof and the floor are left. The BLM did a partial restoration in 1991. The structure is good protection for boaters caught out in bad weather. The cabin is visible from river level, and may be used as shelter on the first night of a river trip.

Nearby Battle Bar was the site several battles (hence its name) in the Rogue River Wars.

Mule Creek Ranch and Museum

Originally homesteaded in 1887 by George Billings, this ranch was a boarding house, post office and general trading post, up until 1931 when Stanley Anderson purchased the ranch and used it as a vacation home. In 1970 the Bureau of Land Management purchased the ranch and began restoration work.

The BLM has restored the ranch and has opened it to the public as a museum. Photographs and artifacts of the history of the Rogue canyon make a pleasant diversion before the whitewaters of theMule Creek Canyon.

Allow some time to explore the Mule Creek Ranch, either as a spot for a lunch brake, or as a campsite on the night before hitting Mule Creek and Blossom Bar.

Self Support

The Rogue is the ideal river for a self-supported kayak trip. Common wisdom says that a multi-day trip has to be done with a raft, big groups, and monumental planning and logistics. However a self-supported trip offers flexibility, freedom, and simplicity of logistics that a raft supported trip can't even come close to matching. Gone is the searching and scrambling for a rafter willing to haul a bunch of kayakers' gear. Campsites that aren't big or flat enough for raft parties are perfect for the small self-reliant kayak group.

On our first self-support trip on the Rogue, we were looking to make camp late in the day, with all the "good," major sites already occupied. We pressed on, and found a small gravel bar near Plowshare rapid. We got out of our boats and found it to be an excellent site for our group of four. The larger, raft supported groups passed it by.

Because of the forgiving nature of the Rogue, this trip is the perfect introduction to self-support paddling. The trip can be made in two days, or three days, but four days are probably ideal. A four day trip allows for a more reasonable pace with time to enjoy the scenery and the river experience. The increase in weight and bulk that must be carried is minimal. Once you have the basic personal and community gear needed for an overnight trip, the only incremental weight and bulk is food, and a little bit of fuel for the stove. Another benefit of small groups is permits are easier to get.

There are many kinds of stow floats or bags on the market today. My favorite is the *Bruneau Bag System from Colorado Kayak Supply*. In my opinion this system offers the best solution for keeping gear dry while minimizing the effect of weight in the boat. If packed properly, these work! I have seen these bags keep a down sleeping bag dry, even after numerous swims.

When planning meals, keep things simple. Try to make meals a one pot dish. Avoid greasy or oily foods; this will ease clean up chores. Nearly all meals can come from the supermarket. Repackage boxed items in heavy duty Zip-Lock bags. Also avoid easily crushed food or packaging.

By choosing and packing your gear and supplies carefully, a self support trip can be made without sacrificing either comfort or fun. The entire river experience is heightened was a sense of commitment and self sufficiency. With the possible exception of a supply of cold beer, there is very little the well prepared self support group has to do without.

Typical busy scene at Grave Creek put-in.

Packing Tips

In order to keep the effect of extra weight to a minimum, the most important thing to remember is to keep the heaviest items close to the center of the boat. Pack the heaviest items, such as cookware or your water filter towards the cockpit. Lightweight items should go towards the end of the boat. By minimizing swing weight, (weight placed at the ends) boat performance should suffer the least. When selecting your gear, be ruthless in your determination of whether you really need it. You should be able to make a three day trip in total comfort and with plenty to eat with about twelve pounds extra.

The following is a list of suggested equipment for a summer or early fall self support trip on the Rogue. Try to make every piece of gear serve more than one function. For example, a paddling top and waterproof paddling pants can serve as rainwear. If you are brave and make a spring or winter trip, modify the list accordingly.

Equipment List

- Boat
- Paddle
- Helmet
- Spraydeck
- PFD
- Stern storage bags
- Bow flotation
- Throwbag

Personal Gear

- Expedition weight capilene or fleece pants
- Capilene top
- Fleece jacket
- wool, fleece, or neoprene socks.
- River sandals
- Wool or pile hat
- Rain pants
- Sleeping Bag
- Bivy bag, ground cloth, tarp or ultralight tent

- Thermarest Pad or foam pad
- Thermalounger (I'll always make room for it.)
- Lexan spoon
- Plastic bowl
- Plastic cup

Community Gear

- Stove
- Fuel
- Cook Pot
- Scrub pad
- Biodegradable soap
- Water Filter
- First Aid Kit
- Matches or disposable butane lighter

Repair Kit

- Duct Tape
- AquaSeal
- Sewing Kit
- Swiss Army Knife or Leatherman tool
- Garbage bag—a large ziplock should do.
- Breakdown paddle
- Safety Gear

Toilet gear

- Plastic trowel
- Toilet Paper
- Heavy Duty ziplock bags
- Lime

Campsite List

Below is a list of the campsites recognized by the BLM and the Forest Service, and is provided for planning purposes only, as all are first come, first served. Generally, these campsites are suitable for larger, or raft supported groups. Many other possible camping site, exist, not included here,and they are adequate for a small or self-supported group. All are accessible from the river, and some are accessible from the Rogue River Trail as well. Note that campsites are not marked along the river, and some campsites may share a toilet with the adjacent location. (Size designation of the camps is that of the BLM).

Note: Most bear encounters are near Tate Creek, Solitude Bar, and Brushy Bar

Campsite	River Bank	Toilet	Size	Miles From Grave Creek	Miles To Foster Bar
Sanderson's Homesite	R	N	L	.8	33.4
Rainie Falls	R	Y	L	1.7	32.5
Whisky Creek	R	Y	L	3.1	31.1
Lower Whisky	R	N	L	3.2	31.0
Doe Creek	L	Y	L	3.6	28.6
Tyee	R	Y	L	4.3	27.9
Wildcat	L	Y	L	5.1	27.1
Big Windy Creek	L	Y	L	8.2	26.0
Little Windy Creek	L	Y	L	9.3	25.1
Jenny Creek	L	Y	L	10.1	24.1

Campsite	River Bank	Toilet	Size	Miles From Grave Creek	Miles To Foster Bar
Horseshoe Bend	R	Y	L	10.5	23.7
Lower Horseshoe	R	Y	L	10.7	23.5
Meadow Creek	R	Y	L	11.5	22.7
Dulog Creek	L	Y	L	11.9	22.3
Kelsey Creek	R	Y	S	13.0	21.2
Lower Kelsey	L	Y	L	13.2	21.0
Battle Bar	L	Y	L	13.9	20.3
Hewitt Creek	L	Y	S	14.8	19.4
Missouri Bar	L	Y	S	16.0	18.2
Quail Creek	R	N	S	16.4	16.0
Long Gulch	S	Y	S	17.0	17.2
Mule Creek East	R	Y	L	19.5	14.7
Mule Creek West	R	Y	L	19.6	14.6
Gleason Bar	L	Y	L	23.1	11.1
Busted Skillet	R	N	S	23.2	11.0
Lower Paradise	L	Y	L	24.3	10.9
East Creek	L	N	L	26.0	8.2
Brushy Bar	R	Y	L	26.1	8.1
Brushy Bar Creek	R	Y	L	26.3	7.9
Solitude	R	Y	L	26.8	7.4
Lower Solitude	R	Y	L	27.1	7.1
Tate Creek	R	Y	S	28.2	6
Lower Tate Creek	R	Y	L	28.2	6
Camp Tacoma	R	Y	L	28.3	5.9
Lower Tacoma	R	Y	S	28.4	5.8
Clay Hill	R	N	L	29.2	5.0
Flora Dell	R	Y	S	30.5	3.7

Lodges

A number of rustic lodges are located on the Rogue River. All require reservations. While most accommodations are booked by guided fishing trips, it is sometimes possible for a private group to arrange a stay. Call or write for more information or to make reservations.

Black Bar Lodge
P.O. Box 510
Merlin, OR 97532 (503) 479-6507

Marial Lodge
P.O. Box 1395
Grants Pass, OR 97526 (503) 479-4923.Ext 7718
(May 15 – November 10) (503) 474-2057

Paradise Lodge
P.O. Box 456
Gold Beach, OR. 97444 (503) 247-6022 or (503) 247-6504

The Lodge at Half Moon Bar
P.O. Box 10
Agness, Or. 97406 (503) 247-6968

Clay Hill Lodge
P.O. Box 18
Agness, OR. 97406 (503)247-6215

Wild River Lodge
P.O. Box 18
Agness, OR. 97406 (503) 247-6215

Approved Outfitter List

This list includes approved whitewater outfitters (as of 1993). This list includes primarily rafting and kayaking. For the most current approved list, contact the Rand Visitor Center.

American River Tour Association
Star Route 73
Groveland, CA 95321 (209) 962-7873

Beaver State Adventures
4430 Lavern
Klamath Falls, OR 97603 (503) 884-7587

Echo River Trips
6529 Telegraph Ave
Oakland, CA 94609 (510) 652-1600

OARS. Inc.
P.O. Box 67
Angels Camp, CA 95222 (209) 736-2924

Orange Torpedo Trips
P.O. Box 1111
Grants Pass, OR 97526 (503) 479-5061

Oregon River Outfitters
1715 Winter St. S.E.
Salem, OR 97302 (503) 363-2074

Outdoor Adventures
P.O. Box 91
Bayside, CA 95524 (707) 830-5114

Rogue River Raft Trips, Inc.
8500 Galice Road
Merlin OR 97532 (503) 473-3825

River Adventure Float Trips
P.O. Box 84
Grants Pass, OR 97526 (503) 476-6493

River Trips Unlimited, Inc.
4140 Dry Creek Road
Medford, OR 97504 (503) 779-3798

Rogue River Trips, Inc.
4186 Normandy Way
Eugene, OR 97405 (503) 344-9024

Turtle Rafting Company
P.O. Box 313
Mt. Shasta, CA 96067 (916) 926-3223

Southern Oregon Raft Trips
14894 Galice Road
Merlin, OR 97532 (503) 479-8508

Sundance Expeditions
14894 Galice Road
Merlin, OR 97532 (503) 479-8508

White Water Warehouse
625 N.W. Starker Ave
Corvallis, OR 97330 (503) 758-3150

Whitewater Voyages
P.O. Box 20400
El Sobrante, CA 94820 (510) 222-5994

Wild Water Adventures
P.O. Box 249
Creswell, OR 97426 (503) 895-4465

Wilderness World
P.O. Box 1647
Grants Pass, OR 97526 (503)479-9554

Supporting raft at Wildcat Rapids.

Managing Agencies

The Wild and Scenic Rogue is co-managed by the USDA-Forest Service and the Bureau of Land Management.

For river information, and private permits contact:

Rand Visitor Center

14335 Galice Road

Merlin, OR 97532 (503) 479-3735

May 15 through October 15: Open 7:00 a.m. to 4:00 p.m., seven days a week.

B. L. M. - Medford District Office

3040 Biddle Road.

Medford, OR 97504 (503) 770-2200

Open year around from 7:30 a.m. - 4:30 p.m., Monday - Friday

For information regarding fishing regulations and licenses:

Oregon Department of Fish & Wildlife

2501 SW First Avenue

Portland, OR. 97207 (503) 229-5403

River History

The first inhabitants were two different groups of Indians, the Tutuni and the Takelma. They spoke different languages, and led entirely different ways of life.

The Tutuni lived along the coast and inland somewhat along the river. They lived in large, permanent villages. An abundance of food, primarily salmon and shellfish was available year round.

The Takelma were semi-nomadic, and moved around in search of food. Their diet consisted of roots, berries, and whatever game they could find. The Takelma lived in middle Rogue Valley and along the banks of the Illinois River.

Early White Visitors

The first non-natives to see the Rogue were English and Spanish explorers coming across the Rogue where the river meets the ocean at Gold Beach. Later, in the early 1800's fur trappers began to explore the Rogue's canyons.

Through the 1830's and 1840's there was not much activity in the Rogue Valley. This was probably the result of the reports of Alexander McLeod, leader of the 1826 Hudson's Bay Company expedition. He reported a scarcity of beavers, and confirmed the reputation of the generally hostile Indians. This quiet spell ended with the occurrence of two events.

Late in 1850, Congress passed the Land Act of 1850. This land giveaway of 2,500,000 acres brought thousands of settlers into Oregon and the Rogue Valley. And with the discovery of gold in 1850 on Josephine Creek (a tributary of the Illinois), and in 1851 near Jacksonville, a flood of outsiders came to the region, and led to the beginning of prolonged period of "Indian troubles."

From the time gold was discovered to 1855, most disputes were sporadic and isolated. Tensions escalated in September 1855, when an Indian attack in the Siskiyou Mountains left two white men dead. Fights and confrontations increased. Attacks back and forth led to what became known as the Rogue Indian Wars of 1855-1856.

The Rogue Wars were a series of battles between the Indians and the Army, culminating with a battle at Big Bend, in May of 1856. Finally the Indians were defeated, and relocation to reservations began. After this sporadic conflicts continued off and on to 1857. These consisted mainly of bounty hunters and government agents tracking and killing remaining holdouts. By the end of 1857 the Rogue River Indians had been completely removed from their ancestral land.

Even after the Indians were gone, the rugged landscape of the Rogue Canyon kept settlement at a minimum. Travel was slow and arduous. Miners were the principal inhabitants of the rugged canyons of the Rogue. Weekly mail service came to the lower Rogue in 1895, with a run from Gold Beach to Big Bend. About the turn of the century, fishing (gill netting and seining) for salmon was the principal industry along the Rogue. The Great Depression brought a renewed interest in gold to the Rogue Canyon. Some of today's place names are from this era. Huggins Canyon and Rainie Falls are examples of names from this time.

1915 saw the first 'whitewater' trip from Grants Pass to Gold Beach. This trip, and the man who made it probably had the most profound effect on the Rogue River in recent times. In a home made boat built of cedar planks and 2X4's, Glen Wooldridge left Grants Pass and made the first successful river trip through what would later become the Wild and Scenic Rogue. This opened up more fishing on the river, and word spread quickly of the Rogue's tremendous fishing. In the following years, more people learned of the excellent hunting and great fishing, including authors Zane Grey and Jack London. The Rogue became a world famous destination.

Glen Wooldridge began to guide many of the newcomers down the river. Tourism became big business, ultimately leading to the closing of commercial fishing in 1935.

Early River Runners

More than any other single person, Glen Wooldridge had the most lasting effect on the river. Glen was a pioneer of the Rogue's whitewater and one of the first and most prolific guides. In the early days of river running, the Rogue was much wilder than today, and equipment and skills were not on the same level of today's as well. Portages were numerous and strenuous. At Blossom Bar, the portage took an entire day. To easy these problems Glen and his cohorts dynamited every significant rapid on the river, from Galice to Agness.

During the 1930's and 1940's, the early river runners blasted a clear channel using a dynamite and blasting powder, often provided by the Forest Service. It was this blasting that made so many of the rapids on the Rogue big, glassy tongues dropping into haystacks and standing waves. Old photographs of Blossom Bar show a nearly impenetrable boulder maze; today the rapid involves a couple of moves and some boulder dodging.

The methods used were not scientific or overly planned. The "river engineers" loaded a sack with rocks and dynamite, ran up close to the offending boulder, lit the fuse, dropped the sack, and then would "get the hell out...fast!."

Blossom Bar is the most famous of the rapids that were changed, but with the exception of Mule Creek Canyon and Devil's Stairs, *every rapid on the river was blasted*. At Kelsey Falls, the big boulder blocking one side of the river (the old channel) used to be in today's main channel.

In his book, *A River to Run*, Glen describes in greater detail the early days and river blasting.

Geology

—An Overview—

The Rogue finds its headwaters on the north slopes of ancient Mount Mazama—today's Crater Lake. From these high elevations, the Rogue begins its 200 mile journey to the Pacific Ocean. As it makes its way downstream it picks up numerous tributaries; the Applegate River and the Illinois River are the largest.

The river takes on many personalities through its downhill trek. High in its watershed, the river is a small mountain stream, similar to many in the Cascade Range. As it cuts its way through the volcanic rocks, it has created spectacular gorges. Northeast of Grants Pass, the river passes under the Natural Bridge, a feature where the river drops through a natural tunnel, disappears underground, and reappears some 200 feet later.

The Rogue is impounded along its course to the ocean as well, taking on a more civilized look. The most significant of these is Lost Creek Dam, built in 1978. Savage Rapids Dam near Medford, and other diversion dams in the Rogue Valley provide water for irrigation.

The river takes on a lazier character as it flows through the Rogue River Valley, near Medford and Grants Pass. Generally, flat sections are punctuated with easy riffles.

As it leaves Grants Pass, the Rogue begins to cut a deep canyon through the Siskiyou Mountains. To the geologist, these mountains are the Klamath Mountains, which generally run from about Roseburg to the north, along the coast south to about the California border. While they appear to be part of the Coast Range, which parallels the Cascades to the east, they are distinct and unique from the true Oregon Coast Range.

Geologically, these mountains are some of the most complex in Oregon. Ocean floor sediments, volcanic activity, and plate tectonics all combined here to make the physical geography of this area an interesting and informative story, and gives insight into the human forces of settlement and exploitation of natural resources. Indeed, the presence of ore minerals (principally gold) was the major force in early white man activity in the Rogue's canyons.

Some 200 million years ago the geologic forces began to form the Klamaths. Tectonic plate movement began stuffing ocean floor under the lighter continental plate. This collision of plates stuffed the heavier sea floor rocks deep into the earth, and crumpled the lighter continental crust into tight folds, forming the Klamath Mountains, the Wallowa Mountains, and the Blue Mountains of northeastern Oregon. These three ranges were formed at roughly the same time, and formed the western margin of the North American continent as it existed at that time. It is particularly interesting to note that the Klamaths in their early days were some 50 miles to the east and south of their present location, and were a part of the growing Sierra Nevada mountains of California. Thus, the Sierra Nevada, Klamaths, Wallowas, and the Blues were one contiguous chain of mountains which made up the Coast Range of prehistoric times.

The Klamaths are made of seafloor sediments and andesite. The presence of andesite indicates that a chain of volcanic islands were offshore from the prehistoric coastline of the continent. These islands may have been similar to today's Aleutian Islands. As the Pacific plate collided with the North American plate, these sediments and volcanics were crunched and crumpled upwards forming mountains. Intense heat and pressure altered these rocks into the hard, metamorphic rocks seen today. Granitic intrusions into the complex added even more spice to the mix.

Between 100 and 150 million years ago, the Klamaths began to drift away from the Sierras, moving to the north and west. At this time they became an island in the sea, offshore of the early continent. Around 50 to 60 million years ago, the mainland and the Klamaths were reconnected, as the separating seaway filled. At about 35 million years ago the mountain building process here came to an end, and the forces of erosion took over.

It appears that the Rogue River existed even during these prehistoric times, and resisted the uplift maintaining its westerly course. The Rogue and the Umpqua to the north were the only rivers in this part of Oregon to keep their original course. All other rivers flow north towards the Willamette Valley.

Geology along the Wild & Scenic Section

From the put in at Grave Creek to the Foster Bar takeout, the Rogue flows through four geologic provinces or formations. The rocks found along the way are some of the oldest in Oregon.

The Galice Formation is exposed at the put-in. Some 15,000 feet thick, this formation is primarily mudstone, laid down in an ancient seabed. Also included in this formation are shales. In places the shales and mudstone have metamorphosed into slate and phyllite, both plate like in structure.

Shortly, the river traveler encounters the Rogue Formation. This formation is volcanic in nature, a result of lava and ash flows that occurred approximately 150 million years ago. This formation too, is thousands of feet thick. Metamorphic heat and pressure altered the rocks of the Rogue Formation. Rainie Falls shows the hard, resistant nature of these rocks. Gneiss is most abundant, while a variety of other metavolcanic rocks are shown here as well. Veins of epidote, a pale green mineral, and black crystals of amphibole can be seen, as well as intrusions of serpentine.

The next twenty miles of the Rogue flows through the Dothan Formation. These rocks were laid down during the Cretaceous period, between 60 and 100 million years ago. The sandstone, mudstone and siltstones here are up to 18,000 feet thick. In many places these rocks are visibly bent and folded, evidence of the forces which created the Klamaths Mountains.

Just below China Bar, the Rogue Formation reappears. Mule Creek Canyon is an ancient fault line, with Dothan Formation rocks on river left, and the Rogue Formation on the right.

Just below Mule Creek Canyon, the Riddle Formation appears briefly. This 80 million year old formation supplies the huge boulders that make up Blossom Bar. These sandstones and conglomerates continue to Clay Hill. Near Clay Hill the Flournoy Formation appears.

The Flournoy Formation of marine sediments continues to the Foster Bar take out. This formation is made of sandstone and siltstone, with some conglomerates. These cemented gravels are prominent along the Clay Hill Stillwater section. This formation is the youngest seen along the river—about 50 million years old.

Wildlife and Plants

Fish

The abundance of fish in the Rogue River is what originally made the Rogue famous. The Rogue's clean water and abundant food source have made it one of Oregon's most productive fisheries.

Unfortunately, like so many of the Northwest's rivers, the Rogue's fishery has fallen victim to over-fishing, mining and logging. In recent years fish are not as abundant as in past times, however the fishing can still be excellent. For more information and pertinent regulations, contact one of the many guides, or the Oregon Department of Fish & Wildlife.

Prominent fish species found in the Rogue are listed below:

Steelhead

Probably the most famous and sought after of all in the Rogue is the Steelhead. Long thought to be a sea-run rainbow trout. In 1988, The Committee on Names of Fishes, of the American Society of Ichthyologist & Herpetologists met to formally vote on the scientific name and classification of the Steelhead.

The Committee decided that the Steelhead, known as *Salmo gairdneri*, would henceforth be known as *Oncorhynchus mykiss*. This re-classification has some significant implications. First, this places the Steelhead as a Pacific salmon, not a trout. Second, this means that instead of the Steelhead being a sea-run rainbow trout, the rainbow is a *landlocked Steelhead*.

This debate undoubtedly continues today. Fortunately, this debate has had no effect on the fish itself, and the Steelhead remains one of the most beautiful, sought after fish in the world.

Chinook Salmon

The Rogue supports two runs of this Pacific salmon. Coho salmon (Silver) also are found in the Rogue.

Sturgeon

This is the largest fish found in the Rogue. This fish can weigh upwards of 1,200 pounds. It is found in the deepest parts of the river, such as the big eddie at Mule Creek.

Other

Native trout can be found in the Rogue and in the various side streams and tributaries. Shad and Lamprey also inhabit the Rogue's waters.

Mammals

The largest of the animals along the Rogue is the Black Bear. Black bear can be any color, ranging from blond-tan to dark black.

They can be seen anywhere, but are most common downstream of Horseshoe Bend, and in particular near Brushy Bar, Solitude Bar, and Tate Creek. Generally these animals keep to themselves, but they have learned about the relation between humans and an easy meal. The most important rule to follow in bear areas is to keep all food out of tents and sleeping areas.

The following tips have helped in keeping "bear problems" to a minimum.

Keep your camp as clean as possible. This means minimizing food scraps, and keeping garbage picked up as well. Some say to hang food and garbage between two trees, at least 12 feet above the ground.

Other tips include:

- Leave a lantern lit all night
- Place small bowls of ammonia on ice chests and dry boxes.
- Tie all ice chests and dry boxes together in one big, awkward block.

Other mammals found in the rogue canyon are black tail deer, raccoon, river otter, roosevelt elk, coyote, cougar, bobcat, skunk, ring tail cat, porcupine and various squirrels and chipmunks.

Reptiles

The Rogue is also home to various reptiles; most are harmless, with the exception being the rattlesnake. The Timber Rattler is the species found in the Rogue Canyon. Common sense usually works to keep you safe from these creatures, however, know the proper first aid in case of a bite.

Be aware that scorpions and ticks are also found in the Rogue canyon.

Birds

Numerous birds make the Rogue their home. For more detail and help in identification, take your Peterson Field Guide along on your trip. Listed below are some of the more prominent residents:

Great Blue Heron
Red-Tail Hawk
Bald Eagle (often seen in the Watson Creek/Big Bend area)
Osprey
Common Merganser
Canada Goose
Kingfisher
Water Ouzel (dipper)

Plant Life

Vegetation along the river varies as the river progresses downstream, and also depends on northern or southern exposure. The north facing slopes typically have denser, more lush vegetation, while south facing slopes support smaller and fewer plants.

At Grave Creek, the plant life reflects the generally drier conditions than downstream, past Mule Creek. Typical of the drier conditions are the oaks, Madrona, and manzanita. Further downstream, trees that are dependent on more rainfall become prevalent. Trees found here are:

Western Red Cedar
Port Orford Cedar
Hemlock
Ponderosa Pine
Douglas Fir
Red Alder

Wild Azaleas and various berries can be found below Mule Creek. Blossom Bar gets its name from the numerous azaleas which bloom in the spring.

With increasing moisture, many varieties of ferns can be found. Look in shady, moist areas for these plants.

Be aware that Poison oak grows in many places along the Rogue. It can be identified by its shiny leaves, in groups of three. Its leaves are dark green, which change to shades of red and yellow in the fall.

Other Nearby Recreation Oportunities

While the primary focus of this guide is whitewater, Southwestern Oregon offers numerous diversions for either the non-boater or as a sideline when in the area for a Rogue trip. Within a couple hours driving, a wide variety of adventures await those who wish to pursue them. Oregon's only National Park, Crater Lake is easily reached from the Medford–Grants Pass area. From the Foster Bar take-out, the spectacular Oregon coast is a short ways away, and can make for an interesting alternative route for boaters heading north.

Other than whitewater and Crater Lake, perhaps the most famous attraction in this corner of the state is the annual Shakespeare Festival. Held every year since 1935, this outdoor festival has grown to a point where nearly 350,000 people attend, over a nine month season. For complete information and schedules, contact:

Oregon Shakespeare Festival
P.O. Box 158
Ashland, OR. 97520
(503)482-4331

Ashland offers a wide variety of food and restaurants, from French Cuisine to Mongolian Barbecue. Main Street is a good place to look for food or a place to stay for the night. Check out the Rogue Brewery and Publichouse (31 Water Street) for hand-crafted micro brews.

The Adventure Center in Ashland can book any number of adventures, ranging from bike tours to horseback rides and river trips. Reach them at (800) 444-2819 or (503) 488-2819.

North, up the road a piece, is Jacksonville. This old mining town has a rich history, and today is somewhat of a tourist town, with a cable car and boutiques and the like. Jacksonville has its own summer-long festival—The Britt Festivals. This musical festival spans a wide variety of musical styles; everything from Mel Torme to country western. Call (800) 882-7488 for more info. Pioneer Days is a Western festival held in mid-June.

Medford is the largest town in this part of the state, a community of about 50,000. Medford provides a complete assortment of Motel 6's, McDonald's and all of the other "modern" conveniences, including two big shopping malls. Medford also is the gateway to Crater Lake National Park.

Follow the signs from town which eventually lead to Highway 62, the Crater Lake Highway. The highway traces a path under the volcanic rock mesas known as Table Rocks and then winds its way further into the forested Cascades. Here many opportunities for hiking, fishing or picnicking present themselves. Many guidebooks and maps present the multitude of choices in this area; to discuss them all is outside the scope of this guidebook. Only the highlights of the area are listed here.

When the highway brings you to the small hamlet of Prospect, try to take time for visit at the Prospect Hotel. This hotel, built in 1889, was host to such luminaries as Zane Grey and Teddy Roosevelt. Dinner is served in the rustic dining room.

Many forest service campgrounds are available for campers, and the Rogue River in this area is protected by Wild and Scenic Status. One of the many scenic highlights is the Rogue Gorge and the Natural Bridge. Here, the Rogue has cut a dramatic defile in the volcanic rock, and plunges through a two hundred foot long lava tube.

Crater Lake National Park is soon reached on Highway 62. Crater Lake is a flooded volcanic caldera, and is the deepest lake in America.

At over 1,900 feet deep, it is the seventh deepest lake in the world. Expect to pay a fee to enter the Park.

For information about the park contact:

Park Superintendent at Crater Lake National Park
P.O. Box 7
Crater Lake, OR 97604

Between Medford and Grants Pass, the little town of Gold Hill is home to the gravity vortex of the House of Mystery. Big signs on the freeway tell you all about the wonders of the House. I am not sure how anyone traveling through the area could miss this mysterious display of natural phenomena.

Grants Pass is touted as the gateway to the Rogue, the Oregon Caves National Monument, and home of some cavemen. Check out the big Caveman statue when you come into the main part of town off Highway-5.

Grants Pass has a complete selection of fast food and motels. A Motel-6 is conveniently located on Sixth Street, close to the freeway. The Mexican restaurant across the street has pretty good food and margaritas.

For Jet Boat tours of the Rogue between Grants Pass and Galice, through Hellgate Canyon, call either Hellgate Jet Boat Excursions (800) 648-4874 or (503)479-7204, or Jet Boat River Excursions at (503) 582-0800.

Southwest from Grants Pass on Highway 199, Cave Junction is the true gateway to the Oregon Caves, and offers a few places to eat and to stay. The Forest Service maintains an office here for information and maps of the surrounding area.

Back to Grants Pass and north up Interstate-5, The Wolf Creek Tavern is definitely worth a stop. This historic roadhouse was a stagecoach stop for the Oregon Stage Company. Signs off the freeway direct you; it is hard to miss.

A rustic restaurant and hotel are the services offered here, and are decorated in the style of the last century.

Across the freeway and up the road a few miles is the old town of Golden. Only a few dilapidated buildings, an old church, and a general store remain.

Roseburg is the closest town of any significant size north of the Rogue put-in along Highway-5. You can find pretty much all you need in terms of fast-food or cheap motels.

State Highway-138 takes out of town, following the North Umpqua River. Best known for the superb fishing, the Umpqua offers whitewater as well. The *Soggy Sneakers Guide* gives complete details regarding these runs. Numerous forest campgrounds are available for camping, contact the Umpqua National Forest in Idelyld Park at (503)498-2531 for maps and information. Susan Creek Campground, administered by the BLM is right on the river and is rumored to have hot showers available.

Scenic Watson Falls, at 272 feet high, is the second highest in the state, and is easily reached from the highway via a short hike.

Farther up the road is one of my favorite spots in Oregon, Umpqua Hot Spring. This is a unique soaking pool carved out of the soft mineral rock deposits left by the spring. Volunteers have built a three sided shelter which overlooks the river below. The water flows from the spring at near 108° F. I will not divulge all the details, but suffice it to say that if make it to the Toketee Lake campground, you're close. Get a good map and good luck.

Back to the Foster Bar take-out, the Oregon coast is only 25 or so miles away. This part of the coast is some of the most scenic in Oregon. What seems to be zillions of State Parks line Highway-101, and motels and restaurants are easy to find.

Gold Beach, named for the early discovery of gold here, is a full service tourist community. Here's the place to catch a ride on one of the big jet boats that you encountered on your trip on the Rogue. Two of the biggest boat companies are Jerry's Rogue Boats (503) 451-3645 or Rogue River Mail Boats (503) 247-7033. Prices are in the $30 to $65 range, depending on length, meal options, etc..

Beachcombing, hiking and fishing are activities found in the Gold Beach area. If you are traveling with a non-boater, this is a good place to share some of your time with them.

In Port Orford , a few miles north, the Prehistoric Gardens seems like a sure bet—where else can you find full-size cement dinosaurs? What better way to round out a Rogue River float trip?

The rest of the beautiful Oregon Coast needs no fancy adjectives to justify a trip through it. Just take your time, come over to see it for yourself, and you'll know what I am talking about!

Camping near Wild and Scenic Rogue

Probably the most common meeting place for Rogue paddlers is the Almeda Bar Campground. This campground is just a few miles downstream from the River Information Office, and features a large parking area for boaters, a big launch ramp area, and a really neat sign warning of all the dangers likely to be encountered on the river. Hazards and dangers like rapids and reversals are described in alarming detail.

The campground has toilets, water, and at last visit, for lack of a better term, raft inflation facilities. A fee is charged, of course.

Farther upstream, the Indian Mary Park is an outstanding campground, a favorite of the motorhome travelers for its excellent location, and perhaps, the availability of hot showers. Another campground run by Josephine County is on Grave Creek near Wolf Creek off Highway 5.

Farther south, is Valley of the Rogue State Park, near the town of Rogue River. This park offers full hookups and shaded grassy sites.

Hiking along the River

For those more inclined to hike than to float, The Rogue River Trail parallels the river from the Grave Creek put-in to the Foster Bar take-out. This trail is along the north side of the canyon, so it gets full exposure to the summer sun. Many hikers make this a four or five day trip The trailhead is at the end of the parking lot at the Grave Creek boat ramp.

The Rainie Falls trail also begins at Grave Creek. This four mile trail follows the left bank as far as Rainie Falls—the trailhead is just before were the bridge crosses the Rogue at Grave Creek.

Maps and more information about the trails may be obtained by visiting the River Information Office.

Selected References

Alt and Hyndman, *Roadside Geology Of Oregon.* Mountain Press Publishing Company Missoula, MT.

Arman, (with Glen Wooldridge) *A River to Run* 1982 Wildwood Press. Grants Pass, OR. 97526

Calabi, *Trout & Salmon of the World.* 1990 The Wellfleet Press. Secaucus, NJ 07094

Cassady, Cross, and Calhoun, *Western Whitewater—From the Rockies to the Pacific.* 1994. North Fork Press. Berkeley, CA. 94703

Garren, *Oregon River Tours.* 1991 Garren Publishing Portland, OR 97219

Nash, *The Big Drops—Ten Legendary Rapids of the American West.* 1989 Johnson Publishing Company Boulder, CO. 80301

Palmer, *Endangered Rivers and The Conservation Movement* 1986 University of California Press. Berkeley, CA.

Orr and Orr, *Rivers of the West—A Guide to the Geology and History,* Self Published, Eugene, Oregon.

Ruby and Brown, *Indians of the Pacific Northwest* University of Oklahoma Press Norman, OK.

The Wild and Scenic Rogue. A video by Gayle Wilson Productions 265 Alta Ashland, Oregon 97520 (503)482-2177

Bureau of Land Management and the Forest Service *Rogue River Float Guide.* 1993

Willamette Kayak and Canoe Club *Soggy Sneakers Guide to Oregon Rivers—A Guide To Oregon Rivers* Third Edition 1994 The Mountaineers Seattle, Washington 98134

Quinn, Quinn, King *Handbook to the Rogue River Canyon* 1987 Educational Adventures Medford, OR 97504